Meditations on the Possibility of Romantic Love in the South between Eras of Nuclear Weapons Proliferation

Meditations on the Possibility of Romantic Love in the South between Eras of Nuclear Weapons Proliferation

poems

RD Morgan

Chicago | Los Angeles

Meditations on the Possibility of Romantic Love in the South between Eras of Nuclear Weapons Proliferation

Published in the United States by Match Factory Editions, 2025

ISBN 978-1-966253-05-1 (hardcover)
ISBN 978-1-966253-01-3 (paperback)
ISBN 978-1-966253-04-4 (ebook)

Library of Congress Control Number: 2024926122

matchfactoryeditions.com

Book layout by RD Morgan

Cover art and design by Gretchen Hasse

Colophon design by Randy Cochran

for Hannah

There are years that ask questions and years that answer.

–Zora Neale Hurston

Table of Contents

two: shadows where the answers wait

one: when there can be questions

The Men-of-War Remained Shriveled in the Sand

I dug my hole. Sat there. Waited
for the tide. Waited for the mud
from my boots to lead me back

to the bars I'd been to, to the days
I'd lost, to the demons
I'd gleefully cross-stitched into sheets.

There were parts of them I hated.
Parts of them I didn't. My black book
swelling on account of humidity and longing.

Pick a Word. Any Word.

Jellyfish.

No.

I saw the holes in his shirt when he pulled it off. He'd spent a week at the beach. Summer vacation. I sat on the tailgate of the pickup.

The blue one, yes. The Mazda.

He nudged the dead rattler with his toe. Watch it, I said. It's still poison. Look, he said, and I did. Touch it, he said, and I did.

Say it.

A Portuguese manofwar isn't a real jellyfish.

No. Say it.

Tangle

It's the waiting that kills me. The incessant freshwater
hum of lemon-scented clouds, compact car

body knowledge, and airbags included for free.
My chemical peel dissolves in my coffee, and I choose

to be naked. Shallow. My greatest fears
involve cliché: weekends waxed with butter-

cream and dun-colored dinner parties.
Goddamn. I say goddamn.

O how a tangle makes me happy! O how the fire
engines blare through the middle of the day!

I rest in lower case. I'm an offseason country
cottage. A structuralist in heat.

O how a tangle keeps my mind busy! O how the ice
cream trucks circle the park each afternoon!

Could the world exist without oranges? Only
mackerel slapped on the table as cast iron heats

in the distance? I rest my case: those harsh remains,
that unrelenting milkjug in the fridge.

This poem steps away

from the window so the cops won't
see. There's trouble on its block
this season, and the door's triple bolted.
Listen: this entire poem is
trouble – an unfiltered pack
of Camels kind of trouble, a triple
vodka tonic hold the tonic thank you
brand of trouble, a briefcase laced
with nonsequential bills piece
of trouble. It's a Harley ridden
on a bad piece of road type
of trouble, and it raises a glass
to the knock from outside.

The Places I Am No Longer Acknowledged

I continued to do my best, limping to some unknown
finish line from a starting point that I —

on good days — referred to as fresh. I was a cargohold
full of dryrot and baggage, and I'd isolated

myself so completely that even the poets
I once called friends no longer remembered

my name on their acknowledgment pages.
I tried hard. I remained calm. Indifferent. My work

colleagues were 22-year-olds who, with eyes full of dun,
earnest wonder, whispered adages like *the right pair of earrings*

will change your life. I was fresh off the tailwind of that awful year
I'd spent flying to a city where I'd never belong. I was tired.

Then you appeared, clutching your losses
so closely they threatened to burn

holes through the remnants of your heart
only one of us believed in.

Time, like a flight pattern, is not linear. I didn't belong
where you were, either.

Somehow, that hurt the most.

I still cannot discuss most things about you.
(*These? They are not tears. They are only water.*)

I want to tell you what you never got to hear: you are
chocolate chip pancakes on a late Sunday morning.

You are dirt bikes gleaming in the unforgiving desert sun. You are
the bright spot in every waiting room.

You are the repainted Camaro in the distance, leaving
me behind, crumpled in the desert

wash, a low-budget rendering of a Wyeth,
my eyes frantically scanning the sky

for anything that could circle
around and connect us again.

Every poem I write closes with a disappearing.
What I never got to say to you: you are

matter in stasis, hovering
in ether, waiting for clearance to land.

> *In the end, I had to find my own way home.*

In the end, rain is really just a cloud falling apart, losing
pieces of itself to rivers, seas, and open windows.

Breakdown

I've come to know the cold. The beer
cans stack up against me like dominoes.

Without you, I am empty, an unmade bed, a form
without substance. A pelican nods itself

to sleep on a distant sandbar. An ice pick
being slipped from a freezer as the lone

taxi makes its way west. The night
sticks on my back like a fistful of fishhooks,

like a pair of hands struggling to regain sense.
The shape of your shadow breaks me. The driftwood

bulkheads remain. I think of the crushed
ice in the corner of the cooler

as a hiding place, a place to place
my heart on evenings like this when even the ocean

perspires. *The curve of your back as you rinse*
sand from your feet at the dunes. There is beer,

there is nonalcoholic beer, and there is tequila.
There is salt, and there is a wound.

Cigarettes snuffed out by the tide. In time,
everything is pulled from the shore to the sea.

There is the scabbing over. A scar.
I think of it as home.

I'm leaving you

the kraken me, the switchblade
in a darkened alley me,
the Stravinsky production
in a back pocket me,
the jagged bolt of lightning
through the window me,
the starving junkyard dog me,
the click of padlock
on the heavy chifforobe me,
the naked power line spitting fire
on the asphalt me,
the lifeless form in the grave
yard lurching closer

Number 14, V. 2

or: after I saw my first Pollock in person at the Tate Modern as my
lover, across the room, wept into his phone

Later that week, at breakfast, hours
before I boarded my international flight home, he felt
in his heart a sudden turn, a sharp shift in direction.
He could relax and finally travel back north
to Nottingham, alone, toward the familiar –
the mindnumbingly monochromatic.

Our pairing may therefore be viewed as transitional.

He feared we'd deadended. That we were no longer
an abstraction. And, on that account, we were no longer.
Absence, after all, had always been our principal element.

The scenes depicted here remain purposefully ambiguous.

A photo taken at Stonehenge shows us in an unfinished state.

His morose mood contributed to my eventual exclusion,
although such a conclusion is speculative.

When he and his wife vacationed in Venice,
he, like Pollock, toured the Matisse Chapel alone. And she
sunbathed: glistening, beautiful, motionless. He never saw me
coming, although he disavowed her months before we met.

In the end, there was no more general agreement.

His favorite poem of mine detailed a relationship's demise.

In the end, there was no more.

I want to believe he did not return to her. I want to believe he continued
to avert his eyes from her presence so that he would not crumble.

In conclusion, there were no set conclusions to be drawn.

I'll remain seared in him
like our shared tattoo, even after
the memory of us grows
dimmer, month after month, finally disappearing:
one last whisper tumbling
over the horizon.

When pressed against the evening sky, all color disappears.

Meditations on the Possibility of Romantic Love in the South between Eras of Nuclear Weapons Proliferation

How he showed you the documentary about the improbability of heartbreak laced up in roller skates, the specter of Burt Reynolds, and Sherman's fiery march to the sea. How he called your kisses sips of laudanum laced with honey on a summer afternoon. How he named you Little Anodyne. How he took your hand and took you down by the river to the colonial town's ruins. How you took him to feed the alligators near the abandoned entrance of the largest munitions storage facility this side of the Mississippi. How he cooked for you most weeks. How the stray ears of corn in the fields, broken and brown, quietly disintegrated to prepare the soil for the cotton's yield increase next season. How you called him on Christmas Eve from the empty sports bar in your hometown. How his line rang and rang as a Godfather played in the distance. How what came from your mouth was not a breath and not unlike a keening

These Are Words Often Used in Combination with Loss

The fact you lost a future. The fact you suddenly lost all
seeds of self-esteem he planted with you.
The fact you continue losing
ounces of yourself each day, as you haven't had heart
or stomach to eat. The fact
your young daughter lost, too.

One single mother knows losing
a partner is statistically inevitable.

Will your daughter's future self vacation on a shore,
look toward the horizon, and remember an impossibly thin
man and his impossibly broad vowels
who, every day, proudly wore the garish
socks she herself selected?

One single mother feels
a sense of loss when her partner leaves
both her and her daughter with one fell swoop
of a fucking phone call.

Fact: your daughter asks about him still.
Fact: even now, even months after
they last spoke, she stands in the surf to lower plastic
ships into the rising tide to sail them to him. To England.

Fact: he lacked
any courage to tell your daughter goodbye.
Fact: his last gift was leaving you
that deed.

Bloom

Did he return to the same spot in front
of the café every day for two weeks?
Yes.

Was he angry when she never returned?
He says that he was not.

What was he thinking during that first week?
*She's got a mean streak in her. She saw me
when she nodded to the postman. She watched me
watching her. I'm sure of it.*

What was he thinking during the second week?
*Give her fifteen years. Those crows will be
perched on her tongue making a nest
of it. She'll try to bite them but just grind
her teeth instead. She'll be that woman
at her neighbor's party. She'll be that
woman following her neighbor's living room
perimeter while balloons pop inside her head
like fireworks. She'll be alone in that
living room double fisting Tuscan reds*

*as her neighbor browns perfectly
rounded patties on his industrial grill.*

***

How many times after their encounter
did she think of himasperson?

Once, soon after, when the postman
did not say hello. She watched his
tiny white truck turn into a tiny white speck,
and then a bug flew into her bangs
causing a bugsized calamity, redirecting
her attention. She checked the mail
then went inside to wash a load of clothes.

How many times after their encounter
did she think of himasaction?
Once, a decade afterward, while shopping for stationery
at the mall. She looked at the fountain in the center
of the food court and remembered it was there, yes,
there, in that exact spot where she saw a stranger
masturbating years ago. She was young. He was
leaning against the fountain looking at her.
His pants: open. His hand: bobbing up and down.
She did not leave while he was there outside.
Afterward, she hurried to meet her mother
in front of Sears. Afterward, her mother
chastised her for being late.

***

First, there is the flower. A flower in a field of flowers,
one half-winged butterfly poised above a green sea.

The undercurrent draws her through the flowers.

Then, there is the flower. Her hands folding
into flowers. Her fingers curling into seas of flowers.

I Keep a Deck of Cards by My Computer to Remind Me

Luck will carry me only so far. I'm no better

than my first high school spring
break, than the first college boy who spread

his cards out on the condo floor and told me
to reach for them. To bend over. That he'd show me

a special game I'd never played before.

Interrogation

Yes, I went there, and I found it dirty: tobacco
flecks in an old purse lining, a construction worker's
steering wheel after five. Yes, I bred an animal,
vigorous and beautiful, a stumplegged horse
sporting aubergine ribbons. Yes, I was poker night,
drawn and quartered. There was no change;

the correspondence between fucking and beauty remained
stale, unimagined: pastel tulips stenciled on a bathroom
baseboard. I was a long letter, yes, that longed to be
opened, hearts scratched in opposing margins
as the hurricane's bright eye loomed unblinking.
Yes, the wind whipped the planters from the back deck,

as the cock and I shattered. Yes, the fucking shifted
toward brute interior: a cologne spill in the corner,
an infected scar from a hot iron. Yes, the scent
of our hands spelled dis-ease. Yes, that cock —
that thin, promiscuous cock! — desired desire,
experience, refined fucking. Yes, it hungered

for carefully shifting dusklight, a glass butterfly's wings.
Yes, that cock was slender, easily broken: a stiletto
dodging sewer grates scattered about,
the rainsogged aftermath of strip poker.
I might have saved us, yes, had my fist not turned
dead, useless, a lighthouse eye after the storm.

Yes. In less than an hour, we drowned.

She Sees the Future Through

She sees the future through the blur
of her arms, knowing the image
of herasaction will soon be forgotten
and replaced by more socially acceptable ones,
like arms swaying in a gentle wind
or arms gently holding babies sleeping.
She wants to snap out of it, to snap off
her skin like a soiled latex glove,
stretch it back on backwards
and use what has been inflicted
upon her to chafe her self into

Seneca Guns and Other Phenomena

Thinking of kissing you, I move
my tongue across my pills.   [my pillow
           dampened by morning's distraction]

Your lips could split an ocean.
O how your mouth broke me!
           [I push the sand grit from my face]

O how you threw me to the unforgiving
Atlantic abyss!   [from the salt smudged window
           I see the pelican, its silent flight above

           the shore reeling against the wind's extensive release]
I am familiar with the sound of cannonfire. The sound
of the Seneca Guns is nearly identical.

           [*could passion be desiring a particular person*
           with a single, mysterious yearning once
           and for always, but always remaining without?]

I hear the windows rattle,
and there is cannonfire in the distance.
The light from the lighthouse throbs with antici

pation. Is it global warming?
Tectonic shifting? Top secret
activity?   [we all have secrets; some of us

stifle them with tetracyclics, assorted candy
colored reuptake inhibitors, and six packs
of diet soda, and when sleep finally comes, secrets

crest then crash over us, leaving us
gibbeted in sweat
soaked sheets come morning]

There is only the invisible
weight of your body rumbling in from the sea, the length
of it stretching over alabaster

lab coats, the whole of its tender
intensity sliding past seismographs.
        [and when I mention pills, I imagine my tongue

        on the cool moonlit seaglass of *bottle*.]
I imagine that one word. That one prayer. That one praise.
That one regret

Apocalypse Provisions

O my little sand clam!
O my velvet corset button!

O my tight shirt donned
at dusk to keep those blues away!

and when my eyes fell on you
I did desire you and when my eyes fell
on you I did then take you
and when my eyes fell on you
I did then hold you fast

O my oversteeped teabag!
O my smelly cigarette stub!

O my missing dresserknob,
my expired medication, my revoked
license, my murderer of crows!

and I clipped my hair today
on account of the moon and the moon
being full I did clip my hair
and my hair being clipped
I did view the moon

Sublimate

Rock bottom at the public pier.
Move around. Get your bearings.
Make yourself useful. Reach
for those boards. They may cover
a treasure. Rip them up. It's easy.
They're rotten, spongy. Like bodies
of creatures pulled to shore.
Smell the old wood. It's you now.
Not even one jewel, or a fistful
of fish scales. Roll up the towel.
Throw it in. Set the wood out
to dry. Then burn.

Emergency Warning

Tissue drifts to the floor
like bad weather. I count
tight pants on television.

Sunday. An old postcard.
I taste an ocean
on my tongue. A room

service bill. Two prepaid dance
steps to the right. Useless
meditations on my last name.

A glossy picture showing me,
that beach, that ship
skeleton, plus evidence suggesting

our marriage was not
wrecked but abandoned.
I mark his face with grease

pencils – blood tears
from a distance. I'll make him
burn. If you could see me

now, before he's come home,
you'd think I'd never been
quite right. You'd see me sitting

in the almostdark, my shadow
on the carpet. It looks
like I am holding nothing

But It's Not for Me to Say

Distant ships hold every woman's wish on board.
A stowaway. Chum trapped in a Styrofoam cooler.

We looked at our feet in the tide pool and then to the ocean.
But it's not for me to say what you were feeling then.

Beneath you I felt uncomfortably small. Human. A lone
sand spur attached to your heel.

That island with the wild horses?
Someone told me they're all gone now. I don't believe it.

I believe they're adapting like the Okavango lions,
on an island in a body of water going nowhere.

.

two: shadows where the answers wait

Category Five

The icemaker sounds a broken
ocean between the shorelines of our marriage.
Our meanings: unmatched, like the quarts of paint
you bought to touch up our walls. You'd tried

to make ~~our home~~ the house for sale
seem less *battle scar* or *testament to failure,*
more *blank slate* for the real estate agent
and her *Tuesday Texas Hold Em* pairs,
and her *Thursday evening casserole* couples,
and her *Saturday night grillout* types –

I turned toward you, and the wind
whipped smoke from the smoldering debris.
The lake slowly crept in from the backyard,
my Diet Coke cooling my neck, the faint half-flush
along my throat having been frosted over for years,
and this time of year being ripe for wildfire, and I
dryrotting inside, and I had not even been

feeling on top of this rubble but standing as if I were

Fundamentals

i.

One reason the sky's blue is not uniform: the air
is denser near the horizon. Scattered molecules
form broken light that the naked eye sees as white.

Even nearsighted, I'm able to see the sky's color
as a plain blue because eyes are more sensitive
to this blue than to its more brilliant violet.

ii.

Our essence is imaginary, yet you and I hide
ourselves with absoluteness: two vertical lines
on either side of an italicized lowercase i: $|\,i\,|$.

iii.

A rational number: the ratio of two
integers with decimals that terminate
or repeat. There must be an endpoint,
or, at the very least, comforting recurrence.

The square root of two is irrational,
just as our root is, both being represented
by approximation. We try to map it precisely
but only smudge it with our whole hands.

32

iv.

For all practical purposes, we cannot prove
i. The essence of real
numbers, however, implies its existence,

even if i cannot be expressed
with quantities of apples or oranges or word
problems like: The milkman

has x milk bottles and gives i
of them to Mrs. Jones. How many bottles
does the milkman have left?

But we yearn for i. We want
i in our lives, even though we can't
touch it. Even though we'll never be able to

explain to a close friend that
i didn't mean to kiss your husband at the office
party last Christmas. It was just that i was under

the mistletoe and *he* happened
to walk past so i, being bold
from eggnog, took advantage

because i was in the right
place at the right time.

v.

The distance between *you* and i can be
calculated. It is growing exponentially.

vi.

As we catch flashes of ourselves
in the heavier air near the horizon,
you plus *i* seems tangible and almost real.

But when the scattered light's recombination
illuminates our appearance, we see transparency.
That our fragility is visible to the naked eye.

Our nearsightedness dictates our far point.
It sets limits on our future, which is not
infinity, but rather somewhere quite near.

Back Porch

No shower.
Only grapes.
Skin softened by saliva
'til there's no more
bitter taste.

Grape pie. Moon pie.
Magpie. Shoo fly.

Her tired body splashes
into clumps of sourweed.

She says out loud a mourning.

She opens cans
of jargon and speaks
freely with them.

Is it any wonder?

About the beer.

How it's never tasted better.

Winter Movement

The winter you left me, I dreamed
I was a bird, a blackbird, a blackbird
blitzkrieg, pure wingvelvet and airthunder.

You folded your hands during sitcoms
while the morphine dripped in time with the earth-
movers six stories below. And my heart

reeked of bar and pool chalk. In the end, my heart
chose broken vending machines over elevators. Loose
change over the chokehold of opening doors.

Fallow

I can still see red. I am not possessed
by a devil. My wound hurts just a little.

Dancing on a screened-in porch.
There was praying after.

What husband.
What farm.

There is nothing to agree to.
No answers. Just a vision.
Where to place my hands
before I die.

Husband, do what you need to.
Go sift the dirt for arrowheads.

The field's my graveyard too.

Barn Burning

Porch swing. The marble angel
stands beside me. I move inside
at midnight to open the closet.
The creatures fall out smelling
like womansblood. They spin
out of the room like lost little girls
in a long-forgotten fairy tale.

I've used diesel; it's a slow burn.
I call the man in the fire
tower to say there's no need to be
anxious.

It's nearly light. I need to tell you
this. Bear with me. I feel
like I'm standing in the middle
of the county fair naked.
I head toward the grain bin
to climb, to jump, then catch light
like a shooting star. Like a falling –

I need
to leave
a permanent mark
on the farm.

I take a wrong step and fall
through the porch and bruise
my shins on magnolia roots.
Rotten wood's no good.

I count the chicken breasts
in the freezer chest to feel
how the frost has hardened them.

I make one wish
before I go
numb

I Want You

The Elks and their fish fries. There's always a fish fry come this time of year. The Elks and their kin continue to dwindle, memberships slowly spiraling toward ground level like silver maple seeds in late spring. Everyone just being so busy. In its previous life, my apartment was an Elks Lodge, and when the wind catches the chimney flue just so, I hear the tap of an empty beer can on the table, the shuffling of Bingo cards. But now my apartment is evolving as I am, one carefully ironed pillow sham at a time. And I am wanting this. I'm wanting this like I want brightly colored cocktails at sunset, or the last ice cream sandwich in the vendor's cooler. I want this for the sake of wanting, like the pilings I want for fence posts, like the backyard I want full of pelicans. I want live music each Wednesday, the dreadlocked bagboy from the island grocery. I want a screen door that opens with a muted click, like a front-clasping bra. I want a mouth on the small of my back that makes me feel like a boardwalk too hot for bare feet, like an ocean crashing over a faded canvas float.

It Was Not Your Fault I Shattered

Sometimes, when I wake up late at night, I wonder if I ever knew you
in another life — we were, perhaps, infants switched at birth
by a sleep-starved nurse, weeknight drinking partners bonding over beer,
or the only two people at the comeback concert who knew all the lyrics.

Maybe we tripped over the same crack in the sidewalk.
Maybe our psychiatrists ordered us both to double our dosages
after the first day of fall when we both crumpled and fell
to our kitchen floors, our hands full of sweaters, tears, and discontent.

Or we could have stayed in the same beach house, years apart,
choosing to play the same words on a warped Scrabble board,
both of us losing in the end as the ocean rumbled dissent in the distance.
Maybe we switched places at one point so it was me crying instead of you,

and you instead of me saying *no one's easy to love every single second,*
and I'd appreciate some goddamn leeway on account of jetlag. Or, instead,
it was your *I love you*, not mine, met with silence heavy as the ocean now
between us. Maybe it was me thinking of that silence, how it became

the wave that capsized and sank me moments before I woke. Maybe you
were the water that freezes, and I was the rock that was broken apart.

Futile Movement

Days since you last fucked. Lights on
in your neighborhood after twelve a.m.
Hours until the milk expires. You count
in fortissimo and spring, turning
your energy outward. You conduct
at night in order to appear. Your theory:

once the female self is no longer
forced into her place, no longer
used for what it is, no longer
fucked – this – the resistance
of insignificance – is more
illuminating than surrender.

Now, with your *own* potency
being acknowledged, with your *own*
staff leaping to you from the podium,
with your *own* baton's base
fitting quite snugly in your palm –
there was little tangible progress.

Only apathy among your colleagues.
You could not even sit with them
at lunch. Instead, you searched
for surrogate institutions. You broadened
your vision. You moved your chair
outside for a different view.

Relax

You chose to be a man today. You can't
find your map. You search for a child
who purposely drops keys. You're late.

You're always late. Now, you can only hear
the creatures as they come
for you. You're worried

about the child. The next time you see
her, she's in a bowling alley
eating pizza. The child: a survivor. You end

up where you started, and then
you're paddling a boat. The paddles splinter
in your hands. You don't know

what you want. You see
light near the end
of a dock, and you hear

scratching under the boat.
You think it's the child,
or the river, so you lean over

Serenata

You can't step into the same river
twice; you have changed, and the river

has changed, so goodnight, Mrs. Calabash,
wherever you are, stripping yourself of day

wear and giving the day's
fragile menagerie of moments extended

release out the window void
of screen. You have looked at the curve

of the river and told of the island it belonged
to, knowing that the shoals would keep it

safe for at least another season, and the sea
gulls' beaks rest aquiver on the day's gentle

seam as it folds over, one single wave
attempting to outlast the shore.

Paperwork

Etched name in dirty oven's ash. Crumbled.

Crumbled petals from corsage collection. Swam over

alligator body in swamp. Smoked stale cigarette

over serial killer's grave. Bit dust on silver

bullet. Drank. Drank from dead man's beer over

his dead body. Avoided. Crouched under. Hid

from. Ran from. Shattered mirrors with bare hands.

Curled up in cinderblock closet. Shaved. Shaved all

number two pencils to nubs.

Threw away photos in a certain way.

Beheaded flowers in neighbor's yard. Charred

pork loins and love notes on charcoal grill.

Incarnate

Women cleaned themselves and pulled
children from the road. Clearly, there
had been a war. I was separated
from the ashes of the dead. I was
nurtured, suckled, sung to. Put on view.
I teethed on severed marble fingers.
I napped in a cracked museum display.
No matter what they did in my presence,
I felt nothing. I never expected that I could smack
my gum in public and have everyone fall
to the floor and start praying. That after a spring
rain, I could open my purse and have dry
cleaning stubs drift to the gutter like dirty manna.
I wanted my body. I wanted to keep
my body until there was nothing left
for the masses to feast on, to pray for,
or to steal. I clawed a shallow hole
inside myself and stilled myself inside
until I could hear screaming.
I left the spot unmarked.

Now Was My Chance

I was institutionalized sufficiently.
I was tired of being
insufficient. How stealthily I noticed

I could finally become!
Now was the time to relax with my loved
ones. They were, of course, incredibly concerned.

The moon was now my cottage, my heavy coat,
my coat-of-arms. My dead of winter, rescued
from the night. My messages that might have been.

Drastic Tactics

In the city with no zip code, the mayor and the councilpersons
gather at the city grill for breakfast. Agenda: non-
linear. Magazines at the eye doctor's office were out
of date. Omelet: extra cheese, no eggs. Steam cleaners
at the grocery store had not been rented for weeks.
Barbed wire around the Girl Scout camp had been snipped
in several places. Double the gravy, no biscuit. The creatures
had begun to rise from the lakes in the daytime.

The next week, a boating accident resulted in paralysis
of the mayor's only child. Which factor – drugs, disgruntled
citizens, or creatures – caused it? The teenager could no longer
apply medicated acne cream. Someone was hired to do this.
Others performed other tasks: speeding past
the police in Drivers' Ed, blasting heavy metal music
during dinner parties, hiding cheap liquor
behind the headboard of the bed.

The lack of iron free water took its toll on the citizens.
Slick red gel appeared around their drains and shower
caddies, around their orifices. Even the finest citizens
looked injured by the sun, as if they'd toiled in tobacco
fields when they were young. The city: quarantined.
Members of the Ladies' Auxiliary traveled door to door: an army
bearing gifts of gingham picnic blankets. The cloth snapped
through the air like a war cry. It covered the ground like a shroud.

We Need You

We need you to focus. We need you to understand
you're on your own. Remember: the old man

in this cafe never touched your cheek or asked how
you were doing. The cook on duty never cared

about your allergy to eggs. Sit down and take a look
at the lot of us: chess pieces lining up at the lunch counter.

We're unraveling the hems of our skirts and pants
with forks and fingernails. We're quite mundane.

Harmless as that glass of water in your hand.
We're knitting a net with our torn threads

Chiaroscuro

Take the man whose eyes, though jaundiced, can still
generate fire. He teaches women to play
pool at two a.m., stretching into the smalls of their backs,
wrapping his cigarette smoke around their restless bodies, leaving
bitter speck of breath behind their ears.

Take the woman who talks with herself, examining her disregard
of sexual vernacular. Shadows wrap the planes of her face.
See how she cannot even masturbate coherently.
Her weight: unevenly distributed.
Her body: imperfectly poised.

Third stanza: an image carved of them
in bed together, her legs spread
predictably. Her marks inscribed on the small of his back:
four paired backward parentheses.

Inventory

The train in the distance was a book I never
finished. I stopped at a gas station, and I was
gushing. All I had: a suitcase of lowcountry

brochures, an assorted inventory
of rods and reels, and a banana peel
from the week before, the smell so sweet

it almost killed me. You said: Absurd!
No rain falls like that! No one sorts her
garbage in that manner! But I didn't pretend

that the ferry floated every bit of the time.
I referred you to the quilt, as it told the whole
story: a roomful of milk jugs, waist high;

a door on the screened-in porch, two
latches. Muted colors and a dust filter.
I was the teenage graffiti on the concrete

pilings. I was the rock hurled at the alligator
twelve feet below. You said: Absurd!
The memory card was full! There is no way

you saved a picture! Yet my point remained
sticky: a watermelon seed spat from a clock,
sweat on a gym teacher's clipboard.

I fought against the whistle, rejected all generics,
for the motel seemed appealing from the outside.
I needed a good cover for the night.

Searching for the Zipless Fuck (Bathroom Break)

It's three a.m. at the bar. You peel your fingernails,
chipping off polish in certain spots to create a rugged look.
A man in a backwards baseball cap follows you
to the restroom because you let him.

You strip your rings off and spread
your hands wide before the door clicks shut, before
he shoves his cock in them. He can't unzip your skirt.
You pull it up.

His back: jammed against the automatic hand
drying machine. It clicks on, off, on again.
The steady hum of hot air turns his back red. He cries out.
The ceiling vent blows winter across your teeth.

A woman outside: knocking.

Backtrack

for Mike Edge

I tried to find my parking space.
It was two a.m. Pines made me feel
wistful, their needles softening

a voice, a whisper in imperative.
An artist snapped his pictures
near the edge. A vision

in the streetlamp's slant of light.
A model scraped her back
against a tree trunk. Harder, I hissed.

Harder. I gave myself up.
Turned around. Resumed my position.
In the bedroom, I lost my balance

when I kissed him. The stress
from his anapests tipped me
out the front door. We lost touch.

Sometimes, skin just doesn't
connect. Sometimes, the pen
isn't held at the right angle

when the boundary lines are drawn.
Trust me: in the end,
the only thing we lost was sleep.

We Move to the Center
for Kelly Hutchison

We are a late night drive after
spring rain. Our headaches collide
headon, and the scented lotion
rests on the endtable, relentless.

There is a black train in our bellies.
There are too many empty nail polish
bottles for our own good. Something
about the glass containers being pretty

on the inside makes us think
about fruit. Plums? Blackberries?
We prefer pomegranates. We are
a red dress. A picture of a pair

of golden shoes. A shadow
from a single bead of sweat.

Carport. A Dozen Grubworms.

The porchlight's fluorescent glow forces them
to shine. Mother-of-pearl. Prescription capsules

that the dogs won't touch. I clean up
the wormtrails. Thick cracks

in the concrete. Company's coming.

Consequence

for George Brown

Whenever I remember you, I think of all
the people in this world who never kept me
warm. I don't mince words; they're all
I have, my gestures being broken, unsuccessful.
Knocks on locked doors, games of chess
I'm forbidden to see.
Your solitary suffering
changed me. My concern turned feral,
toward a perpetual state of not caring
to be known. Toward the brute force
pressing against the pills I take.
A wildness I will never tame.

Open Country

She looks forward to nightfall, when the bed that's awaiting her will renew and refresh her against all these miseries – late night texts from movers, early Sunday morning visits from cable men, real estate agents' stray hands – and, unless she's guilty of some mistake, a bad judgment call at last call – she need not worry about the metes and bounds of her bedsection, for she can stretch across the sheets as far as she dares, in any direction, and roll around as much as she wishes, for she is, for the first time in her tiny, minute life, alone – terrifyingly, splendidly, gorgeously, terribly *alone*. She is, for the first time, eating antacids and Ramen noodles in the same sitting, singing with Elvis at two in the morning, choosing groceries over heat, and stacking books of poems on the dinner table. And this is where we see her, a week before Thanksgiving. She's in open country now, fighting off all the rigors of bad weather – exterminators, deli clerks, lawyers with timid, patient wives waiting at home – armed only with the breath out of her mouth, a breath coming as it does from that dead, empty, hollow place near the heart, a breath that can't help but emerge cold, a breath that, a week before Thanksgiving, formed the words *I am leaving and I am not coming back.*

Unemployed

I pretended to pet the cat. I lied
around the house. I wasn't much.
It was pulling teeth to get me
to say something useful. I needed
a stainless steel springboard.

Cheesecake! I yelled to the wall.
It's all about the cheesecake!
Generally, a smudge above
the couch wouldn't have caught
my attention. It was, however, a leap

year. In time, I altered my ways.
I became a seamstress, dirty
pairs of trousers always on my arm.
In short, I was disgusted.
My tongue became a thumbtack.

Husband, your mother needs help!
Husband, her posterior – it's bleeding!
I scratched my antique table's
underbelly. Played footsie with
Buddy Holly. Cohesive matter

crumbled. Slid through the cracks
like sifted flour. No more Friday checks
to note a week's passing. No more
power lunches. No more teambuilding
with the team who hated me. But still:

I remained hip. I washed my car
in the front yard. I wore my bikini top.
I laughed at the postman's dirty jokes.
I faked a foreign accent.
I was invincible.

Notes

"The Places I Am No Longer Acknowledged" borrows a line of dialogue from the film *The Lobster*.

I incorporated a couplet from the song "Breakdown" by W. Axl Rose into my poem with the same name.

"Meditations on the Possibility of Romantic Love in the South between Eras of Nuclear Weapons Proliferation" takes its name and inspiration from *Sherman's March*, a documentary by Ross McElwee.

I was inspired by multiple passages from *Ulysses* while writing "Bloom."

The closing stanza of "Seneca Guns and Other Phenomena" borrows from Pat Conroy's *The Prince of Tides*.

The italicized stanzas in the "Apocalypse Provisions" were inspired by H. Ryder Haggard's *She* and Joyce's *Ulysses*.

The first line of "But It's Not for Me to Say" is a rewriting of *Their Eyes Were Watching God*'s opening sentence.

I wrote "It Was Not Your Fault I Shattered" after Kim Moore's "In Another Life," which was, in turn, inspired by "The Fair-Haired Farmhand" by Jan Glas. I also borrowed from Jim Harrison's short story "Legends of the Fall" for this poem.

I wrote "Paperwork" as a response to the call of Suzanne Wise's "Fifty Years in the Life of an Aspiring Thug."

"Searching for the Zipless Fuck (Bathroom Break)" was loosely inspired by Erica Jong's *Fear of Flying*.

Phrases and ideas from T.S. Eliot and F. Scott Fitzgerld were borrowed for use in "Consequence."

Acknowledgements

Earlier versions of "Bloom" and "Fundamentals" first appeared in *Third Coast Magazine*. Earlier versions of "Seneca Guns and Other Phenomena," "Tangle," "Interrogation," and "Inventory" first appeared in *Packingtown Review*. Acknowledgements are due to the editors of those publications.

Thank you to my wonderful editor, Snežana Žabić, and to her discerning eye.

Thank you to Chris Adams.

Thank you to Suzan Orrico, whose support has always been invaluable.

Thank you to Shymala Dason, Kathie-Louise Clarke, Allison Burris, and Raymond L. Acevedo.

Thank you to Kelly Hutchison, Mike Edge, Shana Vale, and Emma Bolden. Without them, most of these poems would have remained unwritten.

A special thank you to Beckie Flannagan, Kelly Duke, David Martinez, and Ken Autrey for being my earliest readers.

About the Author

RD Morgan lives in Southern California with her young daughter, and they both appreciate art, sharks, and sea urchins. Much of RD's poetry draws inspiration from the decades she spent in the American South. Her work has appeared in journals such as *Third Coast* and *Packingtown Review*. She holds an MFA in Creative Writing from the University of North Carolina at Wilmington and works as a web marketer for a national nonprofit organization.

www.ingramcontent.com/pod-product-compliance
Lightning Source LLC
Chambersburg PA
CBHW051332120626
46547CB00016B/2500